Contents

Party Time

■ **Listen to the story.**   ■ **Count the letters.**

It's party time.
Some animal friends come to the party
in a bus and a car.

①

Aa

An alligator and an ant bring apples.

②

Bb

A blue bird brings a pie.

③

Cc

A cat brings cookies.

④

Dd

A duck brings ice cream.

⑤

Ee

An elephant brings eggs.

⑥

There are many **fish** in the pond.

7

Everybody has fun.
Everybody eats too much.
A doctor comes to help them.

8

A a

A Say and write.

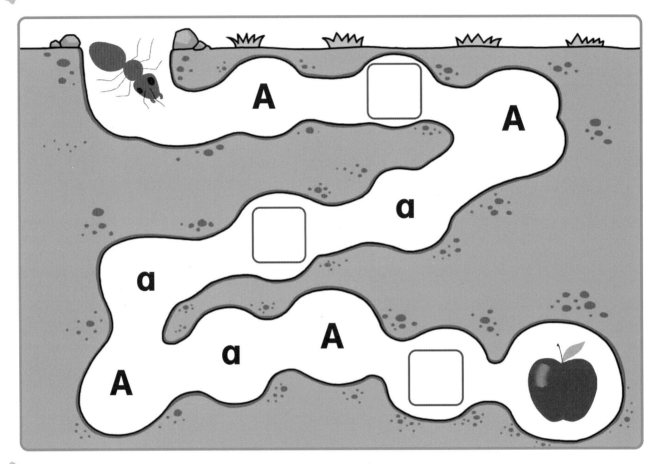

B Trace and write A and a.

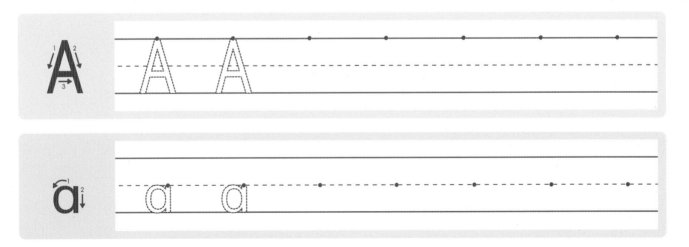

C Say and circle.

1.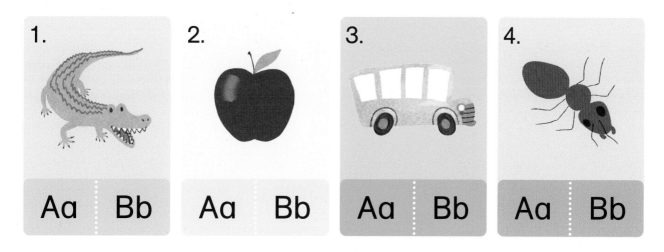

1.	2.	3.	4.
Aa Bb	Aa Bb	Aa Bb	Aa Bb

D Say the sentence. Place the stickers.

An alligator and an ⬜ bring apples.

B b

A Say and match.

B Trace and write B and b.

 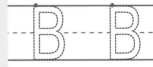

C **Say and circle.**

bird
blue
bus

D **Say the sentence. Place the stickers.**

A blue ___ brings a pie.

Cc

A Say and write.

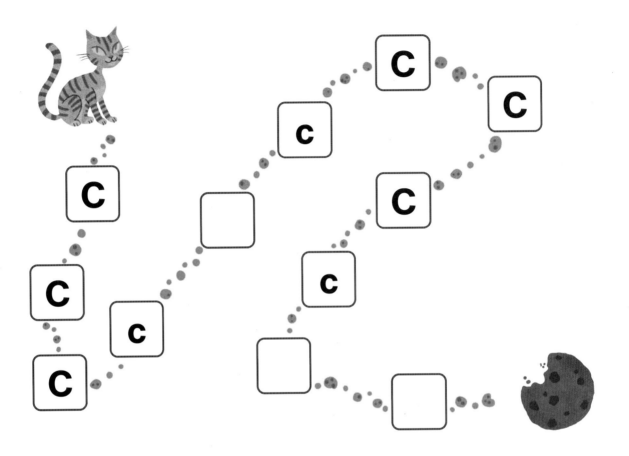

B Trace and write C and c.

C | C C . . . . . .

c | c c . . . . . .

C Say and circle the pictures with Cc.

D Say the sentence. Place the stickers.

A _____ brings cookies.

D d

A Say and match.

1.  • • door

2.  • • doctor

3.  • • duck

B Trace and write D and d.

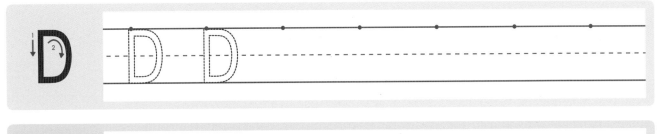

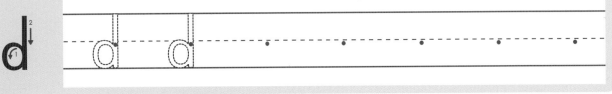

C **Say and circle the pictures with Dd.**

 D **Say the sentence. Place the stickers.**

A _____ brings ice cream.

E e

A Say and write.

B Trace and write E and e.

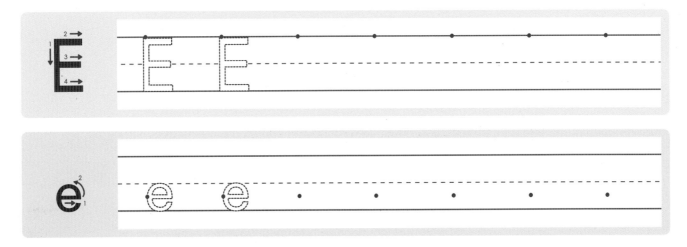

C Say and follow E and e.

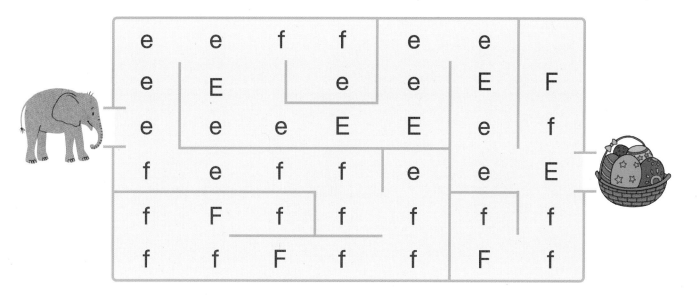

e	e	f	f	e	e		
e	E		e	e	E	F
e	e	e	E	E	e	f
f	e	f	f	e	e	E
f	F	f	f	f	f	f
f	f	F	f	f	F	f

D Say the sentence. Place the stickers.

An _____ brings eggs.

A Say and match.

B Trace and write F and f.

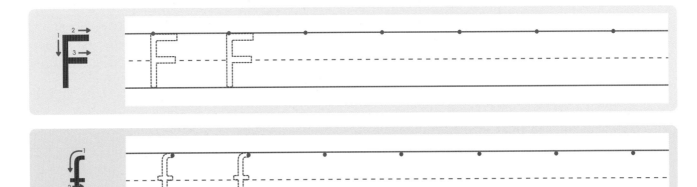

C Say, write, and color.

___an ___ire ___ish

D Say the sentence. Place the stickers.

There are many [ ] in the pond.

A Perfect Day for a Picnic

■ Listen to the story.   ■ Count the letters.

Gg

A girl is standing at a gate.

①

Hh

She lives with a hen with a red hat.

②

Ii

She lives with an iguana with a green hat, too.

3

Jj

She packs apple jam.

4

They go on a picnic.

⑤

Kk

A kangaroo flies a kite.

⑥

The kite sits on a lemon tree.

7

It's a perfect day for a picnic.

8

G g

A Say and write.

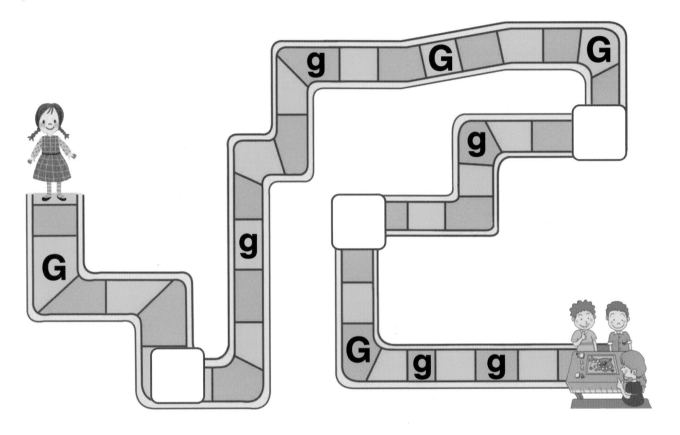

B Trace and write G and g.

G   G G . . . . .

g   g g

C Say and follow the pictures with Gg.

D Say the sentence. Place the stickers.

A _____ is standing at a gate.

H h

A Say, match, and trace.

1.

hat

2.

hen

3.

house

B Trace and write H and h.

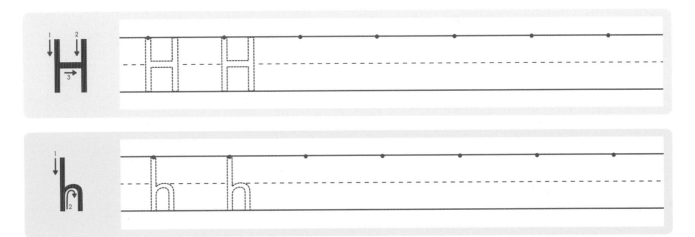

C Say and write the first letters.

1. [ ]ouse
2. [ ]ame
3. [ ]en
4. [ ]at

D Say the sentence. Place the stickers.

She lives with a [   ] with a red hat.

A Say and write.

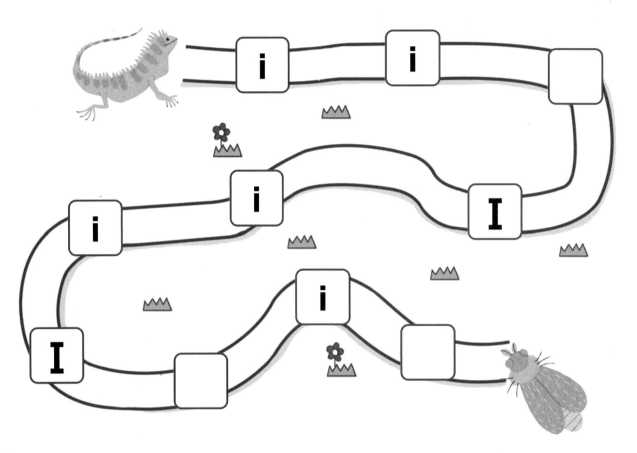

B Trace and write I and i.

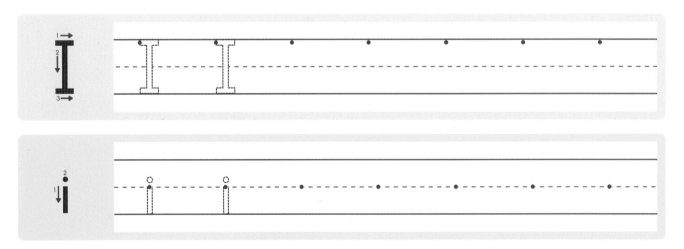

C Say and circle.

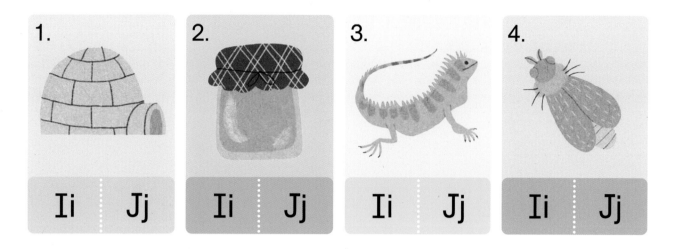

1. Ii | Jj
2. Ii | Jj
3. Ii | Jj
4. Ii | Jj

D Say the sentence. Place the stickers.

She lives with an _____ with a green hat.

A Say and match.

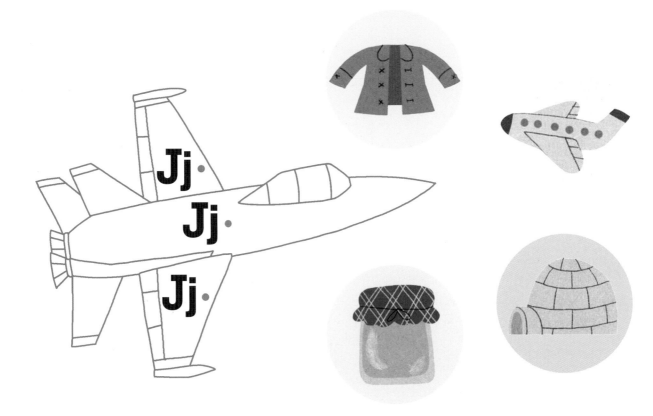

B Trace and write J and j.

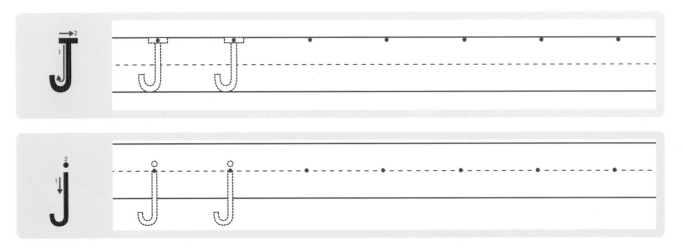

C Say and circle.

jam

jacket

jet

D Say the sentence. Place the stickers.

She packs apple

K k

A Say and write.

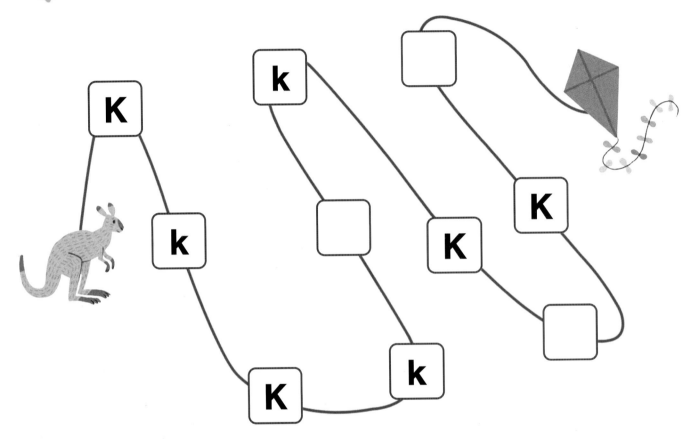

B Trace and write K and k.

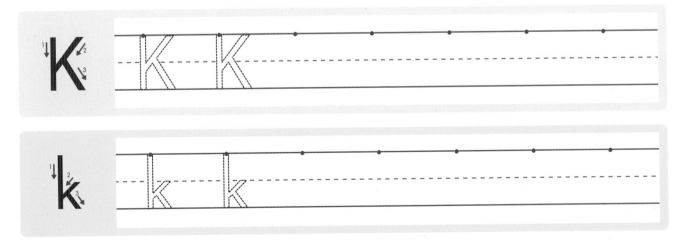

C Say and circle the pictures with Kk.

D Say the sentence. Place the stickers.

A   flies a kite.

L l

A Say and match.

1.

leaf

2.

lemon

3.

lion

B Trace and write L and l.

C Say and circle the pictures with Ll.

D Say the sentence. Place the stickers.

The kite sits on a _____ tree.

- **Listen to the story.**
- **Count the letters.**

Hello friends, do you want a ride?
A monkey with a mask joins the ride.

1

A nurse with a bag joins the ride.

2

An octopus with glasses joins the ride.

③

A pig with a tie joins the ride.

④

A queen with a crown joins the ride.

⑤

A robot with a rose joins the ride.

⑥

Welcome to the trip to the moon!

7

Ten nine eight seven six five four three two one!
The red rocket takes off!

8

M m

A Say and write.

MM mm MM mm

Mm mM Mm mM

B Trace and write M and m.

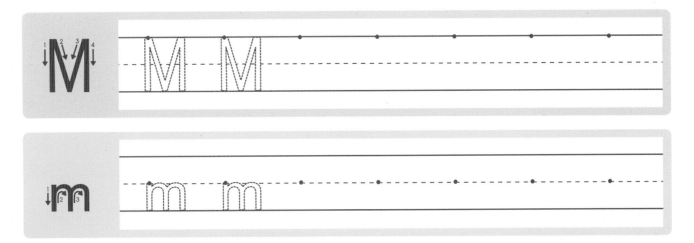

Say and follow M and m.

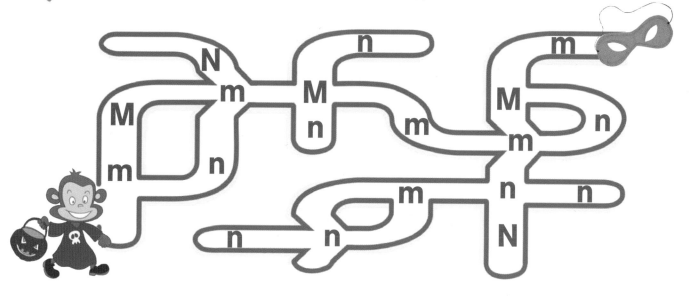

Say the sentence. Place the stickers.

A _____ with a mask joins the ride.

N n

 A Say and match.

 B Trace and write N and n.

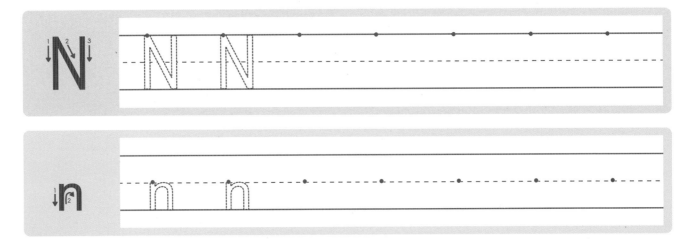

C Say, write, and color.

___ine   ___urse   ___ut

D Say the sentence. Place the stickers.

A ⬚ with a bag joins the ride.

O o

 A **Say and write.**

Oo   oo   oo   Oo   oo   Oo   oo   O___

 B **Trace and write O and o.**

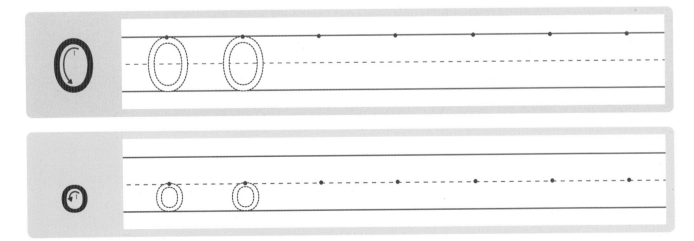

C **Say and follow the pictures with Oo.**

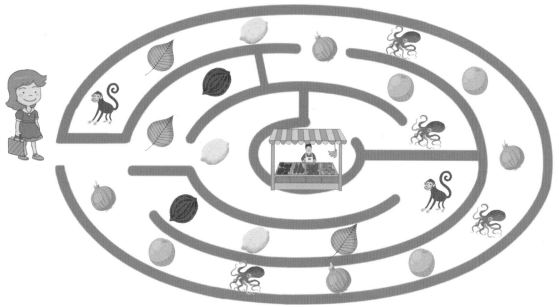

 D **Say the sentence. Place the stickers.**

An _____ with glasses joins the ride.

P p

 A **Say, match, and trace.**

1. 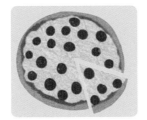 •   • pen

2.  •   • pig

3.  •   • pizza

B **Trace and write P and p.**

P   P P

p   p p

Say and write the first letters.

1. ☐en

2. ☐izza

3. ☐ctopus

4. ☐ig

 Say the sentence. Place the stickers.

A ___ with a tie joins the ride.

Q q

 A **Say and write.**

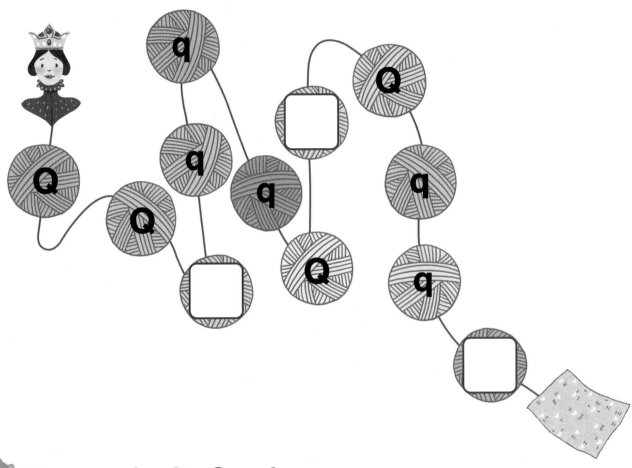

 B **Trace and write Q and q.**

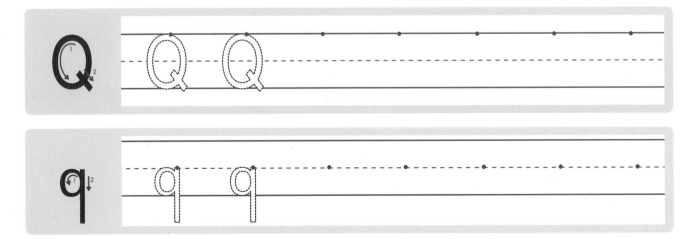

C **Say and circle.**

1.

Qq   Rr

2. Qq   Rr

3. Qq   Rr

4. Qq   Rr

 D **Say the sentence. Place the stickers.**

A [   ] with a crown joins the ride.

R r

A Say and match.

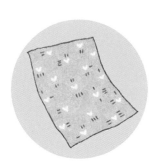

B Trace and write R and r.

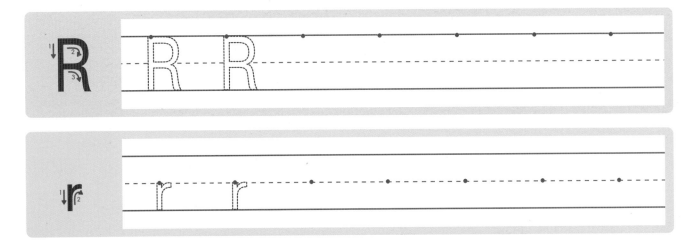

C **Say and circle.**

robot
rocket
rose

 Say the sentence. Place the stickers.

A _____ with a rose joins the ride.

At the Zoo

- **Listen to the story.** - **Count the letters.**

Ss

The sun is out.
A snake is wearing a pink sock.

1

Tt

A baby tiger is playing under a tree.

2

It starts to rain.
"Don't worry!" the unicorn says.
"I have an umbrella."

3

It is a BIG YELLOW UMBRELLA!

4

Ww

A **w**olf comes under the umbrella.

5

Xx

A fo**x** comes under the umbrella.

6

A zebra comes under the umbrella.

7

The sun is out again.
Everyone is happy to play at the zoo.

8

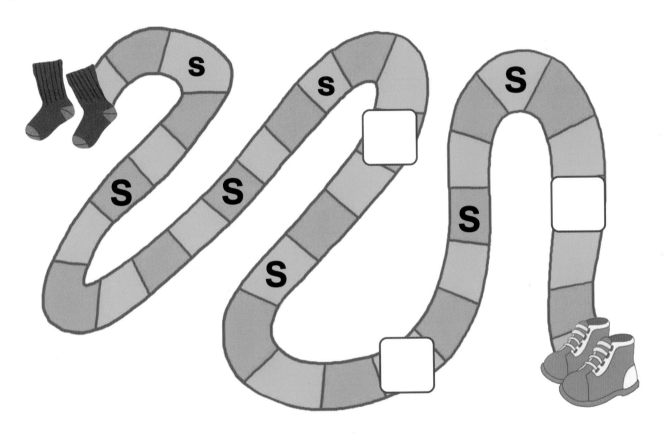

A Say and write.

B Trace and write S and s.

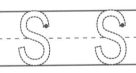

T 23

C Say and circle the pictures with Ss.

D Say the sentence. Place the stickers.

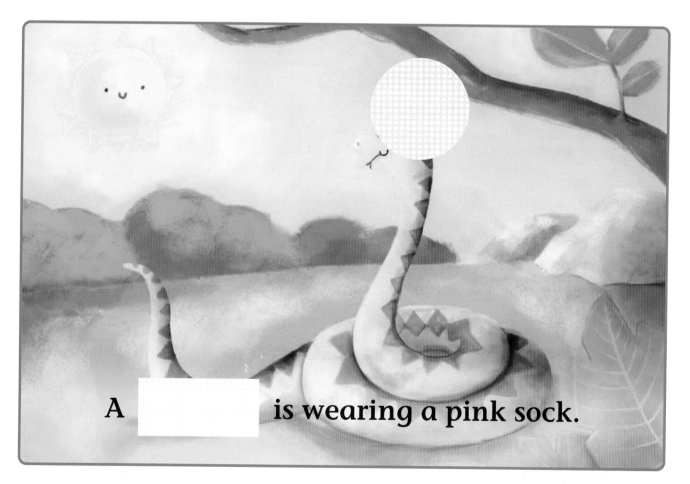

A _____ is wearing a pink sock.

T t

A **Say and match.**

1.  •

• tiger

2.  •

• tree

3.  •

• truck

B **Trace and write T and t.**

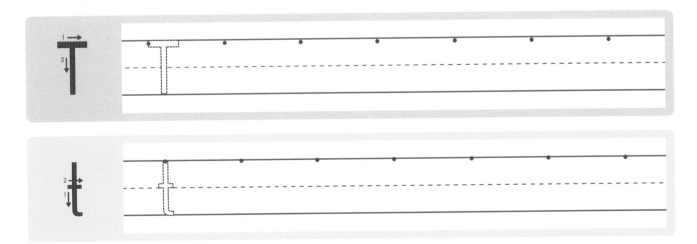

C **Say and circle the pictures with Tt.**

D **Say the sentence. Place the stickers.**

A baby [____] is playing under a tree.

A Say and write.

Uu	UU	Uu	UU	Uu	

VV	Vv	Vv	VV	Vv	

B Trace and write Uu and Vv.

U   U

u   u

V   V

v   v

C Say and circle the pictures with Uu or Vv.

 D Say the sentence. Place the stickers.

"Don't worry!" the _____ says. "I have an umbrella."

Ww

A Say and match.

B Trace and write W and w.

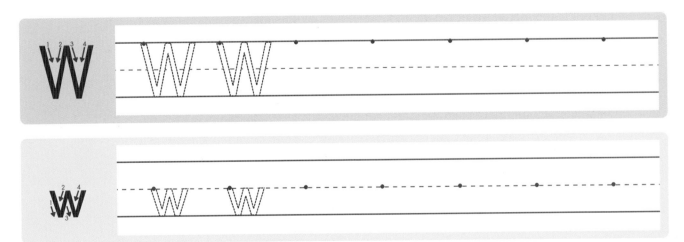

C **Say, write, and color.**

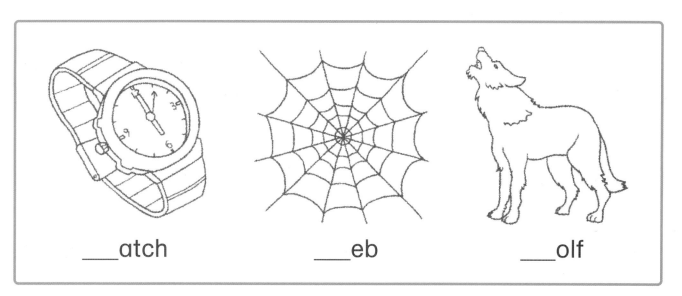

___atch   ___eb   ___olf

 D **Say the sentence. Place the stickers.**

A _____ comes under the umbrella.

X x

A Say and write.

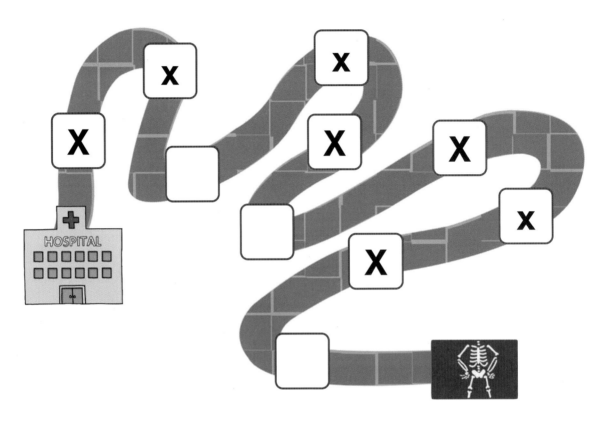

B Trace and write X and x.

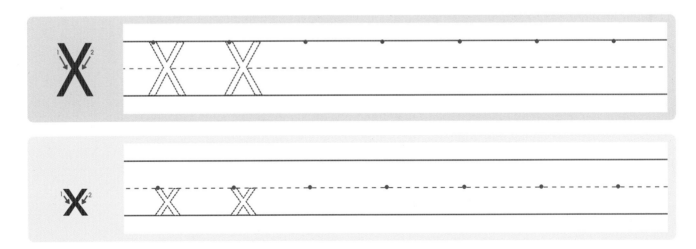

C **Say and follow the pictures with Xx.**

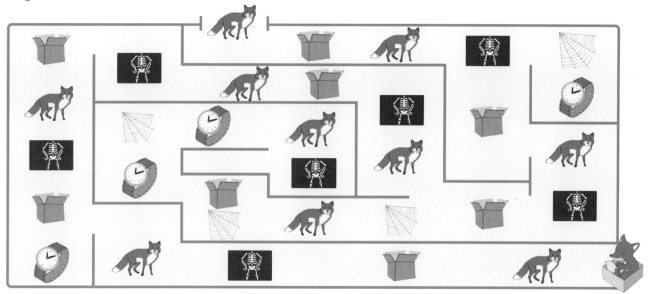

D **Say the sentence. Place the stickers.**

A _____ comes under the umbrella.

Y y   Z z

A Say, match, and trace.

1.  •

• yellow

2.  •

• yo-yo

3.  •

• zebra

B Trace and write Yy and Zz.

 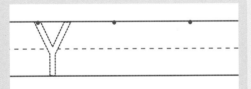

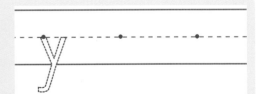

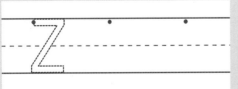

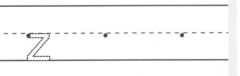

C Say and circle the pictures with Yy or Zz.

 D Say the sentence. Place the stickers.

A _____ comes under the umbrella.

T 29

⭐ **Sing and trace.**

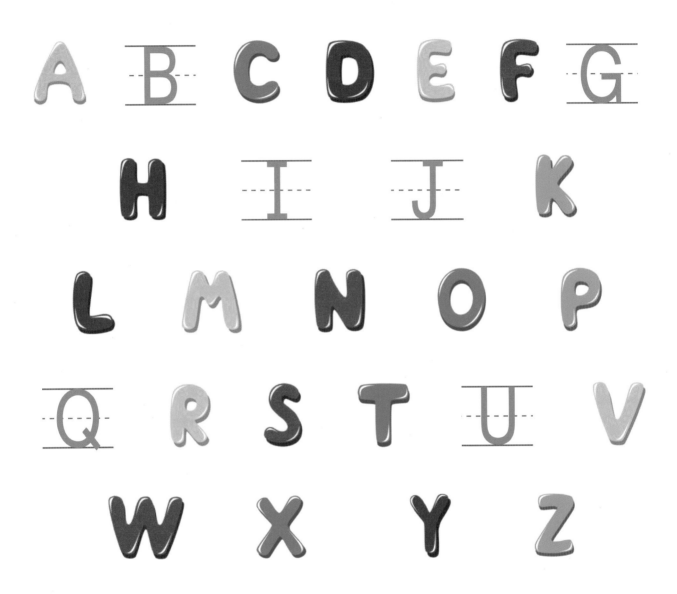

Now I know my ABCs.
Next time won't you sing with me?

Review

⭐ **Say and trace.**

ant

car

door

jam

igloo

game

kite

lemon

milk

octopus

sun

queen

unicorn

x-ray

web

zebra

Unit 1. Party Time

p.2 Aa-7

p.3 Bb-3, Cc-2

p.4 Dd-1, Ee-3

p.5 Ff-1

p.6 **A a**

 a → A → a

 1. Aa 2. Aa 3. Bb 4. Aa

p.8 **B b**

p.10 **C c**

 c → c → c

p.12 **D d**

 1. doctor 2. duck 3. door

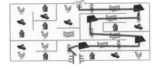

p.14 **E e**

 EE / Ee

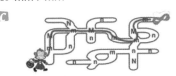

p.16 **F f**

 fan / fire / fish

Unit 2. A Perfect Day for a Picnic

p.18 Gg-3, Hh-5

p.19 Ii-4, Jj-1

p.20 Kk-2

p.21 Ll-1

p.22 **G g**

 G → g → G

p.24 **H h**

 1. hen 2. house 3. hat

 1. house 2. game 3. hen 4. hat

p.26 **I i**

 I → I → i

 1. Ii 2. Jj 3. Ii 4. Ii

p.28 **J j**

p.30 **K k**

 K → k → k

p.32 **L l**

 1. lion 2. leaf 3. lemon

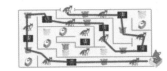

Unit 3. A Trip to the Moon

p.34 Mm-2, Nn-2

p.35 Oo-3, Pp-1

p.36 Qq-1, Rr-3

p.38 **M m**

 MM / Mm

p.40 **N n**

 nine / nurse / nut

p.42 **O o**

 o

p.44 **P p**

 1. pizza 2. pig 3. pen

 1. pen 2. pizza 3. octopus 4. pig

p.46 **Q q**

 Q → Q → q

 1. Rr 2. Qq 3. Qq 4. Qq

p.48 **R r**

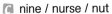

Unit 4. At the Zoo

p.50 Ss-5, Tt-2

p.51 Uu Vv-3

p.52 Ww-1, Xx-1

p.53 Yy Zz-1

p.54 **S s**

 S → s → s

p.56 **T t**

 1. tiger 2. truck 3. tree

p.58 **U u**

 UU / Vv

p.60 **W w**

 watch / web / wolf

p.62 **X x**

 X → x → x

p.64 **Y y Z z**

1. zebra 2. yellow 3. yo-yo

ant	bird	cat	duck
elephant	fish	girl	hen
iguana	jam	kangaroo	lemon

monkey   nurse   octopus   pig

queen   robot   snake   tiger

unicorn   wolf   fox   zebra